# How do I use this scheme?

**Key Words** with Peter and Jane has three parallel series, each containing twelve books. All three series are written using the same carefully controlled vocabulary. Readers will get the most out of **Key Words** with Peter and Jane when they follow the books in the pattern 1a, 1b, 1c; 2a, 2b, 2c and so on.

## • Series a
gradually introduces and repeats new words.

## • Series b
provides further practice of these same words, but in a different context and with different illustrations.

## • Series c
uses familiar words to teach **phonics** in a methodical way, enabling children to read increasingly difficult words. It also provides a link to writing.

LADYBIRD BOOKS

UK | USA | Canada | Ireland | Australia
India | New Zealand | South Africa

Ladybird Books is part of the Penguin Random House group of companies
whose addresses can be found at global.penguinrandomhouse.com.

www.penguin.co.uk   www.puffin.co.uk   www.ladybird.co.uk

First published 1964
This edition 2009, 2014, 2016
Copyright © Ladybird Books Ltd, 1964
001

A CIP catalogue record for this book is
available from the British Library

ISBN: 978-1-409-30129-5

Printed in China

# Key Words

## with Peter and Jane

### 8a
Sunny days

written by W. Murray
illustrated by M. Aitchison

It is summer time. School is over, and the long summer holiday is here.

Jane and Peter talk about their long summer holiday, and what they are going to do.

"I like school," says Peter, "but I am glad the holiday has come."

"Yes, I am glad too," says Jane. "I like sunny days when we have no work to do. There are so many nice things to do in the holiday when it is sunny."

"Yes," says Peter, "and Dad thinks it does us good to get out in the sun. We will be out every day when the sun comes out."

"Do you know there is an old donkey up at the farm now?" asks Jane. "He is too old to work. Pam loves him. We must go up and see him."

"Let's go in the morning," says Peter. "I would like to see the donkey, and we can see the men at work on the farm. Pam may want us to help her."

The children have come to see the donkey. "What a dear old donkey!" says Jane, as she pats him.

"He came last week," she tells Peter. "He came from a place by the sea. Pam found him last week when she was on her summer holiday. The donkey is too slow to work now. Don't get up on him, Peter, he is too old for that."

"No, we must not get on his back," says Peter. "We must look after him. I think he is glad to see us. Pam says he will be here always now. This is a nice sunny place for him."

"Did you bring something for him to eat, Jane?" asks Peter. "We want to make friends with him." Jane has some cake and an apple, and she gives them to the donkey.

"He is not slow when he eats," she says, "but he is slow when he walks."

"We can always see him here," says Peter. "I hope he will be happy here for a long time."

The donkey eats from Jane's hand. Peter pats his head. "He is glad to see us," he says. "I am glad we came."

"What does he do when it rains?" he asks Jane. "Donkeys don't like to get wet. Where does he go at night?"

"They made that little stable for him last week," says Jane. "You can see it over there. He goes to the stable at night and he can go into it when it rains. Let's look at it."

The two children walk over to the stable. The donkey comes with them. "He is not so slow," says Peter.

"He can walk," says Jane, "but he does not like to run."

"Yes, it is a nice little stable they have made," says Peter. "It is just right for a little donkey."

Jane puts her hat on the donkey's head. "If it is too sunny we can make him a hat," she says.

"He likes the sun, and so do I," says Peter. "I hope we have a nice long summer."

The children are glad it is summer. They like long summer days up at the farm. Jane went up last week to have tea with Pam. Now they are going up to the farm house to find Pam. On the way they go by an old barn.

"It is fun to play hide and seek in the barn," says Jane.

"Yes," says Peter, "let's play hide and seek now. You hide first and I will seek."

"Yes, I will hide," says Jane. "Don't look then." She goes into the barn.

Soon Peter goes into the barn after her. He looks for Jane but he cannot see her. Peter goes round the barn again. He looks here and there but cannot find Jane.

Then Jane calls out, "You are slow, Peter, look up here." Peter looks up and sees Jane's head.

"I could not find you. You made me think you were not here. I was going to look in the donkey's stable," he says.

"It would be nice to be up here all night," says Jane.

"We will play once more," says Jane.

"Yes, just once," says Peter. "I will hide now, and you must seek. Don't look, Jane. You must be in here when I hide. See that the door is closed."

He goes out of the barn. He knows where there are some logs of wood, by the end of the barn. He thinks he will hide round by the logs. He goes there at once. "Jane will never find me here," he thinks.

Soon Jane opens the barn door and comes out. She looks round but cannot see Peter. She thinks he may be down by the donkey's stable, so she goes there first. The stable door is closed, so she opens it and puts her head in to look round.

"Not there," she says. Then she runs fast back to the barn. She opens the closed door and goes in. Soon she comes out again.

"Where can he be?" she asks.

Then she sees Peter's head by the logs. "There you are!" she calls out. "I have found you!"

Pam is by the farm house. She looks up at the brother and sister. "So you have come at last," she says. "You have been a long time."

"We had a game of hide and seek in the barn," says Jane. "Peter could not find me, but I found him by the logs."

"We must play that game another day," says Pam. "I like hide and seek too."

Pam has a little black puppy. She is going to give it a drink.

"What a dear little puppy," says Jane. "Let me help you with it, Pam." She helps her friend give the puppy a drink of water.

Then the children play with the black puppy. He runs after them and runs after their ball.

"It is very black," says Peter. "As black as night. You could not see it at night time."

"Did you see my slow old donkey?" asks Pam. "He came last week. He knows how to open and close his stable door. He did not take long to learn how to do it."

Pam tells them how the black puppy got lost last week. "It ran away and was lost all day," she says.

"When I found out I ran to tell all the men the black puppy was lost. Then I ran all over the place to look for it. I ran round so much I got very hot.

"Dad got out the car to help me find it. We went round the farm for a long time. Dad went into the barns and I went into the stables, but the puppy was not there.

"It made me think we should never find it. Then we found it. There it was, down by the logs by the barn. It was the last place we looked."

"What did you say when you found it?" asks Jane.

Pam says, "I said to it, 'You must never get lost again. It makes me think you are lost for always. I don't like it when you are lost.'

"When I got in Mum gave me an ice-cream and she gave the puppy a drink."

"Have you any chicks?" Peter asks Pam.

"Yes, we got some only last week. I went to get them with Dad," Pam says. "Come and see the chicks. They are only a week old. All of them are yellow and they are lovely. We have not lost any."

"I would like to see them," says Jane. Pam takes them to the chicks.

"Look, little yellow chicks," says Peter. "Yes, they are lovely. They have to learn how to eat and drink." They look at the yellow chicks for some time, and talk about them.

Then Pam asks them if they would like some ice-cream. They all want some, so they go back to the house. Pam goes away to get the ice-cream. "Does the ice-cream van call here?" asks Peter.

"No," says his sister. "They make their own ice-cream up here at the farm. It is lovely. I had some last week."

Pam comes back with three ice-creams. The children soon eat them. "Yes, it is lovely ice-cream," says Peter.

Pam takes the children to see her mother's flower garden. There are trees in the garden as well as flowers. There is a wall round the garden and a door in the wall.

"My mother loves flowers," she says, "and she likes to hear the birds sing in the trees. My mother works in her garden every day in the summer.

"She is the only one who looks after this garden. There are many lovely flowers here."

"Look at the big yellow ones," says Peter. "What is the name of the yellow flowers? I like to learn the names of flowers."

"They are sunflowers," says Pam. "I think they have the name of sunflowers because they look like the sun."

"Yes, they do," says Peter.

"Last week when the door was open the chicks ran out here," says Pam. "They got lost, but I went after them and soon found them. It was like hide and seek with them. When we go out we must close the door."

Peter has found a box. In the box are some old school books and some pencils, pens and ink. "An aunty and uncle gave the box to me," says Pam. "We can play with the things in it if you like."

"Let us play at schools, in the barn," says Jane. "We can write in the books and on the wall. There is a big box we can have for a seat."

"Yes," says Peter, "it should be fun."

"Yes, it will be lovely," says Pam.

The three children go to the barn. They make the big box into a seat. Then they take the books, pencils, pen and ink out of the other box.

"I will be the teacher," says Jane. "You do as I say. First I will hear you sing," she says. Pam sings and then Peter sings.

"That is good," says Jane the teacher. "Now we will write. Put your names on the books and then do this." She puts on the wall, "Write a letter in your book."

# Write a letter in your book

The children have a school, with books, pens, ink, and pencils. Pam is the teacher now. She hears the others sing, and makes them write their names. Then she tells them to use their pencils to draw, but not to use the pens and ink.

"Draw a butterfly," says Pam. They do this.

Peter says, "Let us look for butterflies."

"First put the things away," says Pam the teacher. "If you use things you must put them away. Give me the box for the books and the pencils."

"Here are the pens and ink," says Peter. He helps to put the pens, ink, books and pencils away in the box.

"Now you can look for butterflies," says Pam. They see some butterflies on some flowers by a wall.

"Here is a white one," says Peter.

"I can see two white ones, a lovely black and red one, and a yellow one," says Pam.

"Here is one more, so that makes five butterflies," says Jane. "This one is blue. Let them fly away."

Peter and Jane are going to watch Dad play cricket. "I like to watch cricket," says Peter, "and best of all I like to watch when Dad plays. He is good at cricket."

"Dad has a new cricket cap," says Jane. "It is a white one. He uses the white cap because of the sun. He does not use the cap when there is no sun."

Peter gets the new cap. "Dad has put his name in it," he says. Then he says, "Watch me, Jane," and puts the cap on his own head.

"How do I look?" he asks.

"A man's cap is too big for you, Peter," Jane tells him. "Much too big. Take it off."

"Dad has a new cricket bat, too," she says. "I will go and get it."

She comes back with the cricket bat, and they look at it.

"It is a lovely bat," says Peter. "I wish I had a bat like this."

"Yes, it is a lovely bat, but it is much too big for us," says Jane.

It is a sunny summer day. Peter and Jane are going to watch their father play cricket. "Here is the place," says Peter. "It says ENTRANCE. I can read ENTRANCE, and I know what it means. It means the way in."

Jane says, "I can read ENTRANCE, too. Let us go in." As they go in they see the word EXIT. "That says EXIT," says Jane, "I can read EXIT and I know what it means."

"I know, too," says Peter. "EXIT means the way out."

The two children sit down to watch the game. Peter says at once, "That is Dad with the bat. He is the only one in a white cap. He has made some runs, I think. He ran as we came in."

Peter's father hits the ball and runs. Then he hits it once again. Away goes the ball for four runs.

"Dad knows how to use his new bat," says Peter. "There goes the ball again."

"I like to hear the bat hit the ball," says Jane.

Jane likes nothing better than to play with her dolls, but Peter likes nothing better than a good game of cricket. "I like to play, better than to watch," he says.

Today he gets Jane to play cricket with him. "I have nothing better to do," he says, "and you can play with your dolls another time."

Jane says she will play if she can bat first. "Yes," says Peter, "you can bat first. I will soon get you out."

But Jane means to make some runs. She does better than Peter said she would. She knows how to use the bat and she hits the ball many times. At last Peter gets her out. The ball goes under her bat and she is out.

Now Peter takes the bat. He hits out at once and away goes the ball. Soon the ball gets lost. They find it at last, by some logs under a tree.

The game goes on for a long time. Then Jane says, "I want to stop now. I will never get you out."

After cricket Jane says, "One o'clock. It is dinner time." Then they hear Mum call them for their dinner.

"Come on," she says. "Dinner is on the table."

As Jane and Peter sit at the dinner table they think about the afternoon. "What are we going to do this afternoon?" asks Jane.

"You could have a picnic, or fly the kite," says Mum. "Or why not go for a swim?"

"Yes, it would be nice to swim, as it is so hot," Peter says. "Do you want to learn to swim, Jane?"

"I think so," says Jane. "I must learn to swim soon."

"We will all help you," says Peter. "I want to learn to dive. I want to learn to dive under water."

"I don't like it under the water," says Jane.

"Dad and I will come with you, I like nothing better than a nice swim," says Mum. "We'll help Jane to swim and Peter to dive." After they get up from the table, Jane and Peter help Mum.

"I can see that plenty of people are going to the water," says Jane as they go along. "I hope there is room left for us."

They give their money to the man at the entrance and go in. "Is there room left for us?" Peter asks the man. "There are plenty of people here."

"Yes, plenty of people, but plenty of room left," says the man.

They watch other people swim and dive, and then they go into the water. Jane wants to learn to swim, so Mum helps her. Dad dives in, and Peter watches him as he goes under the water. Then Peter dives in, as Dad watches.

"Good!" says Dad. "You will soon learn to dive like other people. There are plenty of days left in the holiday."

"Yes, I mean to learn," says Peter. "On a hot day nothing is better than a dive into the water."

Dad goes to help Jane, and Mum comes to dive with Peter. They have a good time in the water. Then they have tea in the café.

Every year their friends next door go to the sea for a holiday. Year after year they go to a nice place they know well. They like the place and the people there.

This year their friends write a letter to say that the weather was bad at first. Then the bad weather went away, the sun came out and the weather was beautiful.

"It has not been bad weather here," says Peter. "We have had sun all the time."

Mum reads on, "A friend of ours has been made Queen of the Sands for a week. She is a beautiful girl and makes a beautiful Queen. We have a picture of her as Queen. Our children, Bob, Mary and Molly are with her in the picture. You will see it when we come back.

The children have had a lovely time on the sands and the pier. They have been to see Punch and Judy, and Bob went out in a motor boat.

They are going to buy a little present to give you when they come back."

It is good weather for a holiday. The children like to be out in the sun. Their mother comes out and gives them a big box of old clothes. "These are for dressing up," she says. "I know you like dressing up. This can be your dressing up box." Peter and Jane thank her very much and then open the box. They look at the clothes and take them out.

Peter says, "There are big clothes and little clothes, old clothes and new clothes."

Jane says, "There are hats and caps, too. There are red clothes, yellow clothes, green clothes and black clothes. We can have fun with these."

"Yes," says Peter, "these are just right for dressing up."

Mum watches the children from a window. She likes to see them have fun.

"Look Jane," says Peter. "Do I look very old? I am an old man."

"Yes, Peter," says Jane. She is dressing up in some red and white clothes. "I am going to be a Queen," she says. "I am going to be a beautiful Queen."

The children have lots of fun with the dressing up box. Peter says that the box is a boat and he is lost at sea.

Jane says that the box would make a nice house for her dolls, with lots of room for them all. Then she says, "I am dressing up as an old woman now." She goes to let Mum see her. In the room she sees a cup of tea on the table.

"Would you give an old woman a cup of tea?" she says.

Peter hides in the box under some clothes. Jane comes out and she cannot see Peter. She calls him but hears nothing, so she looks round the garden.

Then she says, "He must be in the dressing up box, under those clothes." She runs back to the box and looks in. "Come out from under those clothes," she says.

When he gets out Peter has some red and white clothes. "I can be a Father Christmas with these," he says. "Look, Jane, I am Father Christmas."

Mum looks up from a letter to say, "Your grandmother is not well. She fell down in the garden."

Jane asks, "Was it a bad fall, Mum?"

Mum says, "No, it was not a bad fall. I will read to you, 'Last week I fell down in the garden. I was not well for two days, but I am much better now. I cannot pick the fruit this year and I don't want to see it left on the trees. Would Peter and Jane come over and pick the fruit for me?'"

"Yes," says Peter, "I like to pick fruit. She will let us eat lots of it."

"I like to pick fruit, too," says Jane. "We will be only too glad to help."

As Dad comes into the room for a cup of tea, Mum looks up from the table. She says, "Grandmother fell down in the garden. These two want to pick the fruit for her."

"We will be only too glad to help," says Dad. "We will go over to see Grandmother this morning."

"What a beautiful day," says Jane.

"Lots of lovely fruit to pick," says Peter. "Grandmother says we can eat some."

Both of the children work for a long time, until they have picked a lot of fruit. Then they both stop to watch a beautiful butterfly go by.

"Grandmother makes lots of jam out of this fruit," says Jane. "She gives Mum some of the jam, and sends some to her friends. It is lovely jam."

"Yes," says Peter. "It keeps until Christmas. We had some of her jam last Christmas."

They take the fruit into the house and give it to their grandmother. "You are both good children to help me like this," she says. "I have made a nice tea for you."

After tea their mother and grandmother make some jam from the fruit the children have picked. Peter and Jane watch.

Grandmother talks about her fall. She tells them she is well again now. "You must not fall again," says Mum.

Dad has bought a tent. He bought the tent for both the children to play with, in the garden. Two men came up the road with it this morning. They left the tent but did not wait. The children put up the tent after dinner, but it soon fell down. They got it up again, but it fell down once more.

"We should have asked those men to help us," says Jane.

"Which men?" asks Peter.

"I mean those two men who came with the tent this morning," she says.

"We can do it," says Peter. "You push this, and I will pull. Don't push until I say so. You push now," he says, and he pulls. They both fall down. Down comes the tent again.

"We want help over this," says Jane. "We don't want to push and pull and fall down until bedtime, do we?"

"We must both wait until Dad comes in," says Peter.

"Yes, we can wait until then," says Jane. "I am glad Dad bought the tent," she says.

The children are both going to the park to play with their friends. As they go into the park they see a door which has PRIVATE on it.

"I can read that," says Peter. "It says PRIVATE. It has PRIVATE on it so that children will not go in."

"Yes," says Jane. "When they see PRIVATE, they keep out. That is the house and garden of the man who looks after the park." They both go into the park and play with their friends.

Soon they see Bob and Mary come into the park. They have just come back from their holiday. Bob and Mary tell Peter and Jane about all the things they did on their holiday.

"We were on the sands a lot," they said. "We ran about all the time, but Mum and Dad just sat in the sun. They sat there in the morning and sat there in the afternoon. They both love the sun."

Jane says, "Our Dad has bought a tent for us. We should all have lots of fun in it."

It is the end of the day. It has been a lovely summer day. Peter and Jane have been out in the sun all the afternoon. They have had games with their friends in the park, and they have been with Bob and Mary in the tent.

Now it is time for bed, and Peter and Jane are in their bedrooms. It is hot. Peter goes to his window, and looks out. He can see the red sun as it goes down over the hills. "Come and look at the sun, Jane," he calls. "It looks beautiful."

Jane comes into Peter's room. They both look out of the window. "Yes, it is beautiful," says Jane. "It looks so red at this time of night."

"You can just see the hills," says Peter. "They do look nice like this."

Mum comes into the room. "Back you go to bed, Peter and Jane," she says. The two children run back to their beds.

"Good-night," they say to their mother.

"Good-night, Peter, good-night Jane," she says. "Good-night, my dears."

# New words used in this book

**Total number of new words: 91**
**Average repetition per word: 11**